The Essentials of Financial Planning

Dr. Latson W. Cockfield and James G. Ibe, PhD

Copyright Statement

The Essentials of Financial Planning

Dr. Latson W, Cockfield

Prof. James Gaius Ibe, PhD

Library of Congress Control Number: TX 9-458-361this text or product material

Soft-Cover Edition: ISBN: 979-8-992-1515-0-3

Global Group LLC

595 Rainbow Drive

Sumter, South Carolina, USA

The Essentials of Financial Planning

Preface

Welcome to the exciting world of financial planning. This book is designed to be your comprehensive guide to navigating the complex landscape of personal finance. Whether you are just starting out on your financial journey or looking to refine your existing strategies, the information within these pages will provide you with the knowledge and tools you need to make informed decisions and achieve your financial goals.

This book provides practical guidance on financial planning-based research, principles of finance, and best practices. The principles of finance include the following:

Money has a time value

Higher returns are expected to take on more risk.

Diversifying one's investment can reduce risk.

Financial markets are efficient in pricing securities.

The objectives of managers and stockholders may differ.

Reputation matters and past performance do not guarantee future performance.

In today's fast-paced and ever-changing world, having a solid understanding of personal finance is more important than ever. From managing debt and budgeting effectively to investing wisely and planning for retirement, the decisions you make about your finances can have a profound impact on your future financial well-being.

This book is divided into several sections, each focusing on a different aspect of financial planning. We will start by laying the foundation with fundamental concepts and principles before diving into more advanced topics. Along the way, you will find practical tips, real-life examples, and actionable strategies to help you apply what you have learned to your own financial situation.

But financial planning is not just about numbers and equations, it is also about setting goals, understanding your values, and making decisions that align with your priorities. That is why this book takes a comprehensive approach, considering not only the quantitative aspects of finance but also the emotional and psychological factors that influence our financial behavior.

Whether you are aiming to build wealth, achieve financial independence, or simply gain greater peace of mind about your financial future, this book is here to guide you every step of the way. So, let us embark on this journey together and empower ourselves to take control of our finances and create the life we desire.

Dr. Latson W. Cockfield, DHA, MSFS, CLU, ChFC

Prof. James Gaius Ibe, PhD, CAE, CAM

Florence, South Carolina

Shaw Air Force Base, South Carolina

Dedication

This book is dedicated to people who want to know more about the essentials of financial planning.

Disclaimer

Many individuals and businesses have lost their homes, cars, and businesses by doing financial planning only to find it a waste of time and money. They would have had a better plan if they hired a financial advisor. This is not to bad mouth people; it is to help people change their spending habits and things to look for when choosing a financial advisor.

Please consult a competent professional for specific advice. The following are some general guidelines for wealth creation and personal financial planning.

Acknowledgments:

I would like to express my gratitude to my wife Helen and my children for their knowledge of the significance of studying. Additionally, I would like to express my gratitude to my mother, Pearl N. Cockfield, for instilling in me the value of the Lord and for teaching me to respect everyone. I would like to express my gratitude to the Best Sellers Guide members and my friends for their assistance in writing this book. For his patience with me when I was writing my first book, I would want to credit James Ibe, Ph.D., my former professor, co-author, and editor.

About the Authors

Dr. Latson W. Cockfield, DHA, ChFC, CLU

Dr. Cockfield holds a Doctor of Healthcare Administration degree from Virginia University of Lynchburg and has previous experience working in the insurance industry. He is experienced in business planning, coaching, sales, instructional design, and team building. Dr. Cockfield is a finance expert with a master's degree in financial services, Chartered Life Underwriter, Chartered Financial Consultant designation, and a bachelor's degree in organizational management from Morris College.

Prof. James Gaius Ibe, PhD, CAE, CAM

Dr. James Gaius Ibe is a tenured professor with a wealth of experience in economics, finance, and business administration. He earned his Ph.D. in International Economics from the University of Texas. Dr. Ibe has over 35 years of post-doctoral research and graduate teaching experience in financial management and risk mitigation strategies. He serves as the Chairman/Managing Principal-at-Large of the Global Group, LLC-Political

Economists and Financial Engineering Consultants. His research interests include risk mitigation, financial engineering, fraud examination, and financial cybersecurity. Dr. Ibe integrates extensive industry senior management experience with rigorous academic research and best practices. He has contributed to various fields through publications and teaching, making him a respected figure in academia.

Table of Contents

Chapter 1: Setting Financial

Understanding Your Financial Goals

Short-term vs Long-term Goals

SMART Goal Setting

Specificity

Calculate Your Income:

Track Your Expenses:

Fixed Expenses

Variable Expenses

Discretionary Expenses

Savings and Investments

Analyze Your Spending

Create the Budget

Implement and Adjust

Differentiate Needs and Wants

Avoid Impulse Purchases

Use Cash for Discretionary Spending

Set Spending Limits

Automate Savings

The Most Important Distinctions between Cash Flow and Income

Final Thoughts

Importance of Saving

Types of Investments

Risks and Returns

Aging Clients

Retirement Goals

Strategies for Retirement Planning

Understanding Taxes

Tax-efficient investing

Asset Location

Tax-Advantaged Accounts

Tax Planning Strategies

Qualified Plans

Non-qualified Plans

Rules Regarding Withdrawals

Participation of Your Employer

Required Minimum Distributions

Gift and Estate Tax Planning

Hiring a Tax Professional

Kind of mortgages

The kinds of life insurance policies

Whole Life Insurance

Term Insurance

Universal Life Insurance

Variable Life Insurance

Endowment Insurance

Annuities

The kinds of disability Insurance:

Short-Term disability insurance

Long-term disability insurance

Employer-Sponsored Disability insurance

Supplemental disability Insurance

Hospitalization

Medicare

Medicaid

Property and Casualty insurance:

Homeowners insurance

Auto insurance

Rental insurance

Identify-theft insurance

Umbrella insurance

Flood insurance

Earthquake insurance

Business insurance

Liability insurance

Professional liability insurance

Workers' Compensation insurance

Cyber insurance

Boat and Yacht insurance

Travel insurance

Assessing and Managing Risk

Risk Identification

Avoidance

Transfer

Retention

Reduction

Risk Evaluation

Contingency Planning

Communication and Reporting

Adaptability

21

Training and Awareness

Estate Planning Basics

Assessments

Legal Documents

Reverse Mortgage

Beneficiary Designation

Guardianship

Debit and Tax Consideration

Regular Review and Updates

Looking Back Period

Wills

Trusts

Probate Avoidance

Flexibility

Privacy

Comprehensive Planning

Inheritance and Legacy Planning

Family Communication

Values and Visions

Charitable Givings

Education and Guidance

Documenting Personal History

Memorialization

Professional Guidance

Divorce

Marriage

Birth or Adoption

Loss of a Loved One

Disability

Career Change or Job Loss

Windfall (Inheritance, Lottery, etc.)

Health Crisis

Starting a Business

Educational Expenses

Tax Changes

Global Events (Pandemics, Economic Crisis)

Financial Planning for Marriage:

Financial Planning for Children' education

Financial Planning for Divorce

Insurance Coverage

Comparison Shopping

Retirement Planning

Retirement Age

Market Conditions

Tax Planning

Changes in Tax Laws

Maximize Tax Benefits

Estate Planning

Legal Document

Beneficiary Designations

Professional Guidance

Financial Advisor Consultation

Legal and Tax Advice

Adaptability

Flexibility

Learn and Adjust

Record Keeping

Organizing Documents

Secure Storage

Emergency Adjustments

Immediate Changes

Making an Adjustment as needed

Staying on Track to Achieve Your Goals

Budgeting

Emergency Fund

Debt Management

Insurance

Investing

Retirement Planning

Estate Planning

Financial Education

Setting Goals

Budgeting

Emergency Fund

Debt management

Investment Planning

Retirement Planning

Insurance Coverage

Tax Planning

Estate Planning

Continuous Review

Encourage Ongoing Financial Education

Summary

Regular Reviews

Life Changes

Income and Expenses

Investment Portfolios

Emergency Fund

Debt Management

Insurance Coverage

Retirement Planning

Tax Planning

Estate Planning

Professional Guidance

Adaptability

Record Keeping

Emergency Adjustments

Adjusting as needed

Staying on track toward your goals

The Purpose of the Book

This book, which is named "The Essentials of Financial Planning," was published with the intention of highlighting the significance of financial planning.

I would want to begin by giving credit to the Lord, and I would like to mention that my mother was the one who instilled in me the belief that the Lord exists.

During my childhood in the little community of Scranton, South Carolina, I was always aware of the fact that I wanted to serve in the military. After completing my high school education, I volunteered to join the military and went on to serve for more than twenty years, during which time I was on active duty as well as reserve service. In addition to being awarded the title of Armed Forces Expeditionary, the Army Commendation Medals, and the teacher of the year award, I eventually retired as a Master Sergeant (8). Among my many accomplishments, I was also given the title of commander. After I was discharged from the military, I began working as a financial consultant for both individuals and organizations, in addition to selling a wide variety of insurance policies. On the other hand, I came to the awareness that to achieve a high level of achievement, I would need to get extra knowledge. Because of this, I decided to enroll in The American College of Financial Services. The college provided me with the opportunity to gain credentials in the fields of Chartered Life Underwriter and Chartered Financial Consultant, in addition to a degree in Master of Science in Financial Services. Following that, I went on to acquire a Bachelor of Science degree in Organizational Management from Morris College and a Doctor of Healthcare Administration from

Virginia University of Lynchburg. Both degrees were earned after a few years had passed.

Because working as an insurance agent and Chartered Financial Consultant allows us to interact with a wide variety of people and trains you to become the best in your field, I wanted to write a book on the subject as soon as I earned my Chartered Life Underwriter and Chartered Financial Consultant designations, as well as my bachelor's and master's degrees. The title of the book would be "The Essentials of Financial Planning." I went out to Dr. James Ibe, who had been my professor at Morris College, after I had completed my studies at Virginia University Lynchburg and received my doctorate degree. Following a great deal of discussion, we concluded that we would collaborate on the production of a book that would be titled "The Essentials of Financial Planning." I made the decision to take this action as a response to the fact that I had learned of people, including members of my own family, who had lost their homes, automobiles, estates, and retirement plans because they did not have long-term care insurance. Since I did not have fire insurance for the family home, it was a circumstance that was bad for our family. The house is reduced to ashes because of a fire.

I could not help but think about the house that we lost in a fire, the employees who worked at ENRON when the firm went bankrupt around the year 2000, and the COVID 19 pandemic that occurred during that time. All these things came to mind. Throughout the time that we were working on this book, I could not help but think about all these different topics. On the other hand, we are of the opinion that if they had employed a financial advisor, they would have been able to acquire funds from the insurance company,

ENRON workers would have been able to retire at this same moment, and they would have been able to save a greater number of lives during the COVID 19 pandemic. If a significant number of people had lost their lives and the virus continued to spread, this would have been the result.

Introduction

Financial planning is a necessary activity in which all people young and old should engage. Most people wish to retire to a comfortable lifestyle equal to that which they have become accustomed to during their working years. Many have questioned their present and future financial situation, especially with the financial crisis we are living in today. To prevent anxiety about one's future and finances, it is important for each person to consider the benefit of financial planning. There are several important financial dimensions to be taken into consideration when making short or long-term plans. First, in planning one must consider the various types of insurance needed, such as life, health, accident, property, and casualty. Financial planning will also include employee benefits, pension plans, estate planning, investments, retirements counseling, and risk management. The financial crisis we are living through today has many people asking whether they even need a financial planner or consultant. This all depends on each person's situation. Most people will find that they are better off seeking information, expertise, experience, and discipline provided by a financial advisor. Making quality financial decisions requires commitment to learning by attending the appropriate schools and getting practical experience. Whether a person wants portfolio management to plan for retirement long-term care insurance, or to reach any other financial goal, there are professional planners or consultants who have spent their careers serving people with the same concerns; it is worth a person's time to check out the kind of work involved in financial planning. Many people have tried doing financial planning only to find it to be a waste of time and money. If they had hired a financial planner or consultant, they would have a much better plan.

Chapter 1: Setting Financial Goals

Understanding Your Financial Goals: You must choose short- and long-term goals because knowing what goals you want to achieve in your retirement years is essential. Understanding your financial goals is critical in managing your personal finances and working towards a secure financial future. Here are some key points to consider when determining your financial goals:

Short-term vs Long-term Goals: Start by distinguishing between short-term and long-term financial goals. Short-term goals are typically achievable within a year, while long-term goals may take several or even decades.

SMART Goal Setting:

Specific: Clearly define the goal. It should be precise and unambiguous.

Example: Instead of saying, "I want to improve my health," specify, "I want to lose 10 pounds."

Measurable: Establish criteria for measuring progress and success. This helps track progress and stay motivated.

Example: "I want to lose 10 pounds" is measurable because you can track your weight loss.

Achievable: Ensure the goal is attainable and realistic, considering available resources and constraints.

Example: "I want to lose 10 pounds in three months" is more achievable than "I want to lose 10 pounds in one week."

Relevant: Make sure the goal aligns with broader objectives and is worthwhile.

Example: If improving health is important, losing weight contributes to this larger goal.

Time-bound: Set a deadline or timeframe to create urgency and focus.

Example: "I want to lose 10 pounds in three months" sets a clear time frame. **Prioritization:** Determine which goals are most important to you. You may have multiple goals, but it is essential to prioritize them. Settings will help you allocate your resources accordingly.

Realism: Be realistic about what you can achieve. While it is good to be ambitious, setting attainable goals can lead to satisfaction. Consider your income, expenses, and other constraints.

Time Horizon: Consider when you want to achieve each goal. Some may be short-term (e.g., paying off credit card debt), while others may be long-term (e.g., retirement savings).

Emergency Fund: Having an emergency fund as one of your initial financial goals is admissible. One of the reasons is an emergency fund that can help you deal with unexpected expenses without derailing your other financial plans.

Debt Management: If you have high-interest debt, like credit card debt, consider paying it down as a priority. Reducing debt can free up more money for other goals.

Investment Goals: If you are considering investing, define your goals. Are you saving for retirement, a home, or another long-term objective? Your investment strategy will depend on investment goals.

Retirement Planning: Retirement savings are crucial to long-term financial strategies. Determine how much you need to save and invest for your desired retirement lifestyle.

Education Goals: If you or your children plan to pursue higher education, set financial goals for funding these expenses.

Homeownership: If you want to buy a home, determine your budget, and start saving for a down payment.

Charitable and Legacy Goals: If you have Philanthropic or legacy goals, decide how much you want to contribute to the charity or leave for future generations.

Regular Review: financial goals may change over time due to changes in your life circumstances, priorities, or financial situation. Regularly review and update your goals.

Financial Advisor: Consider seeking the advice of a financial advisor to help you set and achieve your goals. They can provide expert guidance and help create a tailored financial plan...

Automatic Savings: Setup automatic transfer to your saving and investment to make it easier to stick to your goals.

Remember that achieving financial goals often requires discipline, patience, and consistent effort, understanding your financial goals and creating a plan to achieve them is a fundamental aspect of financial well-being. It provides direction, motivation, and a road map for making informed financial decisions.

Chapter 2: Budget and Expense

Budgeting and expense management are crucial to personal/financial health/ planning. Effectively managing your finances through professional assistance helps you allocate resources wisely, save for future goals, and avoid unnecessary debt; here are some steps and tips for budgeting and expense management: monthly expenses.

Set Financial Goals: Determine your short-term and long-term financial objectives, such as saving for an emergency fund, paying off debt, buying a house, or planning for retirement.

Calculate Your Income: List all sources of your monthly income, including salary, bonuses, freelance work, investments, etc.

Track Your Expenses: Categorize and record all your expenses over a month. This includes:

Fixed Expenses: Rent/mortgage, utilities, insurance, loan payments.

Variable Expenses: Groceries, transportation, entertainment, dining out.

Discretionary Expenses: Hobbies, vacations, non-essential shopping.

Savings and Investments: Retirement accounts, emergency fund, education savings.

Analyze Your Spending: Compare your expenses to your income to see where your money is going and identify areas for potential savings.

Create the Budget: Allocate your income to each expense category, ensuring your total expenses do not exceed your income. Prioritize essential expenses and savings.

Implement and Adjust: Regularly review your budget, track your spending, and adjust as needed to stay aligned with your financial goals.

Differentiate Needs and Wants: Focus on fulfilling essential needs before spending on non-essential wants.

Avoid Impulse Purchases: Implement a waiting period before making non-essential purchases to evaluate their necessity.

Use Cash for Discretionary Spending: Limit spending to the cash you have on hand to avoid overspending.

Set Spending Limits: Establish and adhere to limits for variable and discretionary expenses.

Automate Savings: Set up automatic transfers to savings and investment accounts to ensure consistent contributions.

Review Subscriptions and Memberships: Regularly review and cancel any unused or unnecessary subscriptions and memberships.

Shop Smart: Use coupons, shop sales, and compare prices to save on groceries and other purchases.

Prioritize Debt Reduction: Focus on paying off high-interest debt to reduce financial burden and free up more of your income for other goals

.

Chapter 3: Income and Cash Flow

Understanding the most important financial concepts regarding income and cash flow is critical in the beginning of any effective financial planning. Two of the most fundamental ideas in financial management are income and cash flow. These concepts are essential for determining the overall financial health of both individuals and corporations. Both terms have unique meanings and connotations, even though they are frequently used interchangeably. The purpose of this article is to provide an explanation of the distinctions between cash flow and income, as well as their constituent parts and the influence they have on the process of financial planning and decision-making.

Definition of Income and Different Types of Income
The term "income" refers to the monetary amounts

that are obtained by an individual or corporation from a variety of sources. Additionally, it is typically calculated on a monthly, quarterly, or yearly basis. It is a representation of the economic advantage that is achieved over a period. Different forms of income can be distinguished from one another: This is the whole revenue before any deductions or costs are deducted from it. Gross income is also known as "gross income." When it comes to companies, it is the money that is made from selling products-goods, services or ideas to customers. The amount that remains after all costs, taxes, and deductions have been removed from gross income is referred to as the "bottom line," which is another name for net income. Additionally, it reflects the real profitability of an individual or firm. Earned income includes not just wages and salaries but also tips and any other form of revenue that is obtained via employment. It refers to the money that is generated by the core activities of a company. Income that is not directly gained via work or services is referred to as unearned income. This category includes revenue from investments, interest, dividends, rental income, and any other income that is not directly earned. The Significance of Earnings Income is an essential measure of how well a company is doing financially. It is the factor that defines an individual's capacity to pay their living expenditure, save for the future, and invest that is important. When it comes to enterprises, it is a crucial factor in determining the success of their operations, affecting stock prices, and having an effect on the capacity to recruit investors and get financing.

The Definition of Cash Flow and the Components

That   Make   Up   Cash   Flow

The actual movement of money into and out of the accounts of a company or a person is referred to as those accounts' cash flow. This is a measurement of liquidity as well as the capacity to meet costs that are due right away. Cash flow may be divided into three primary types, which are as follows: Operating cash flow refers to the cash that is created from routine company activities, such as the sale of products or services, as well as the cash that is paid for costs such as rent, utilities, and wages because of such operations. A positive operating cash flow implies that the fundamental business activities of a firm are profitable enough to provide sufficient cash for the company to continue and expand its operations.

The term "investing cash flow" refers to the cash that is either utilized for investments in assets such as property, equipment, or securities or is created by such investments. As an illustration, the purchase of a brand-new piece of machinery would be considered an outflow, but the sale of an older asset would be considered an inflow. There are a variety of cash transactions that are associated with financing operations, such as borrowing money, repaying loans, issuing shares, or paying dividends. This category includes all of these cash transactions. A change in the capital structure of the company is brought about by these operations. Value of Cash Flow in a Business Maintaining liquidity and ensuring that a company or a person can pay their short-term obligations both require a steady flow of cash flowing into their accounts. Even businesses that are lucrative have the potential to fail if they do not effectively manage their cash flow. This is because they may not have enough money to pay their debts. The ability to reinvest in the company, pay off debt, and distribute dividends to shareholders are all aspects that are made possible by a positive cash flow. The Most Important Distinctions Between Cash Flow and Income Different insights may be gained from revenue and cash flow, despite the fact that they are related: When it comes to timing, income is recognized at the time it is generated, regardless of when funds are actually received. Cash flow is solely concerned with transactions that involve actual cash. On the other hand, cash flow is a measurement of liquidity, whereas income is a measurement of profitability over a period of time. In contrast to cash flow, which focuses on the amount of cash that is available to fulfill costs and commitments, income is concerned with the overall performance of the company's finances. As an example, consider a company that does business on the basis of credit. The realization of the income occurs now of the sale, which results in an increase in revenue. The cash flow, on the other hand, is only impacted when the payment is received. Because of this, a firm may have a profit (positive income), but it may still experience difficulties with its cash flow if its receivables are not collected in a timely way while it is operating.

Final Thoughts

For efficient financial planning and management, it is vital to have a solid understanding of both concepts: income and cash flow. Income offers a glimpse into the profitability of a business, while cash flow provides an understanding of the liquidity of the business and its capacity to satisfy immediate financial commitments. Both measures are essential for guaranteeing long-term sustainability, evaluating the state of the company's finances, and making educated judgments on matters pertaining to the firm. Both people and companies can attain financial stability and development if they successfully monitor and manage their cash flow and income resources.

Chapter 4: Savings and Investing

Regarding our retirement, the kind of savings and assets we have built are vitally necessary. Saving money and investing are both essential components of personal finance, yet they serve different tasks and should be managed in a particular manner. Investing and saving money are both important components. To provide a concise summary of each, the following is a list of them: These three cost reductions are included in the package: Setting aside one's salary to access it in the future or the event of an emergency is what is indicated by the phrase "savings." Both certificates of deposit (CDs) and savings accounts are examples of accounts frequently used to save money because they are low-risk and easy to access. CDs and savings accounts are two instances of accounts. The primary purpose of savings is to create a financial cushion if unforeseen expenses arise, such as medical emergencies, automotive repairs, or job loss. It is usual practice for financial experts to recommend that individuals construct an emergency fund that is adequate to cover the costs of living for six months. Putting your money into assets to obtain a return over a period is indicated by the phrase "investing." investment is sometimes called "investing." Many different types of securities could be considered investments. Some examples of these securities are stocks, bonds, mutual funds, real estate, and other financial instruments. Whereas savings always involve some degree of risk, investments almost always involve some degree of risk, and the promise of more significant returns typically comes with a higher amount of risk.

Importance of Saving: Accumulate money for wealth and emergency.

We, the two authors of this book, have been studying financial planning for a few years, and throughout that time, we have witnessed a significant improvement in how individuals have increased their savings. Saving is vital for a few reasons, including both short-term and long-term financial well-being. Listed below are some of the most important reasons that show the significance of conserving money:

An Accident Fund: If you have savings, you can establish a reserve for emergencies that will aid in case of job loss, unexpected medical expenses, or automotive repairs. When individuals do not have savings, they may be compelled to resort to debt with high-interest rates or be forced to make difficult decisions regarding their finances during times of crisis.

Monetary Stability and Security: The practice of saving money not only helps you meet your regular needs without relying on credit or loans, but it also provides a sense of security and peace of mind. This financial stability reduces the risk of falling into debt traps, giving you the confidence to face any unforeseen circumstances.

Saving money is not just about financial security; it is also about setting yourself up for future success. Whether your long-term financial goals involve buying a home, starting a business, or exploring the world, saving consistently is the key. It is a practice that can help you amass the resources you need to turn your dreams into reality, instilling a sense of hope and motivation in your financial journey.

Preparing for Aging: Putting money aside for retirement plans is necessary. such as 401(k)s, 403 (b)as well as IRAs. This will allow you to build up a substantial nest egg for retirement.

Possibilities and Flexibility: Having funds allows you to take advantage of these possibilities and be flexible. It will enable you to take advantage of unanticipated possibilities, such as investing in a promising startup or pursuing higher education, without worrying about the limits of your financial situation.

When individuals have suitable saving methods, they often seem less stressed. The effect of stress on one's mental and emotional well-being can be significant when related to financial matters. Individuals can alleviate stress and experience greater peace of mind by starting to save money and having a solid financial foundation. This lets them know they have resources to fall back on if they need assistance.

Economic cycles are unavoidable, with times of expansion followed by periods of contraction. This is the seventh and final point on the list. It is possible to lessen the impact of economic downturns, job losses, or unanticipated financial shocks by contributing to the accumulation of savings during times of prosperity.

Being an Example to Others: To set a good example for future generations, developing and maintaining excellent saving practices is essential. Instilling a sense of financial responsibility in youngsters and preparing them for a more secure financial future can be accomplished by teaching them the significance of saving money.

In closing, saving money is an innovative financial behavior essential to gaining freedom from debt, security, and stability. Because of this, Individuals can negotiate the unknowns of life, follow their ambitions, and construct a more prosperous future financially.

Type of Investments: Purchasing a home as an investment to increase your assets and lower your taxable income. Stocks and bonds are another way of improving your assets, however,

Remember that when investing in an open market, one must think of one's personal and financial levels of risk tolerance. You may need to hire a financial advisor. A regular savings account is one of the basic systematic ways of increasing your assets. One can apply any number of personal or reliable disciplines to achieve success through this method. Weekly, bi-weekly, monthly, or annually for example.

Individuals can also take advantage of IRAs, 401ks, and 403bs, which have savings, tax-deferred, and capital appreciation features.

Risks and Returns: Stocks and bonds, Real Estate. The authors believe that people interested in acquiring something should contact people who are informed about risk and return products, including real estate. In finance, risk and return are two of the most fundamental principles that may be used in different investments, including stocks, bonds, and real estate. When structuring their portfolios, investors must consider the many asset classes, each carrying its own unique amount of capital risk and possible return. Risk: Stocks are considered one of the riskiest asset classes because their prices are prone to extreme fluctuations. Extreme price changes can be caused by various variables, including the firm's performance, the market's sentiment, the economy's conditions, and the occurrence of geopolitical events.

History has shown that stocks have historically offered more significant returns over a long period than other asset classes. This can be accompanied by increased volatility and unpredictability. Over the long term, the average annual return on equities is between 7 and 10 percent. Bonds: Risk Bonds, which reflect debt obligations issued by firms or governments, are often considered less dangerous than equities. This is because bonds represent debt obligations.

On the other hand, bond prices are still subject to change because of interest rate fluctuations, changes in credit quality, and other variables. Return: Compared to equities, bonds typically give lesser returns but provide more dependable income streams. Coupon payments and the possibility of capital gains or losses upon maturity comprise the returns when bonds are purchased. Risk in Real Estate: The risk associated with real estate investments can vary significantly based on many factors, including the location, the type of property, the market circumstances, and the amount of leverage used. Several dangers are associated with real estate, including vacancies, liquidity problems, maintenance costs, and market downturns. Rental property and expenses can be taxed, written off, and appreciated, which could be a significant investment and provide a regular income and the possibility of gain. Income from rentals and appreciation of the property's value are two potential returns that can be obtained from real estate investments. Throughout history, real estate returns have been comparable to equities over the long term, averaging between 8 and 12 percent annually but with substantially less volatility. However, people thinking about investing in bonds, stocks, and real estate would most likely be at a disadvantage, which could be devastating to their retirement.

Chapter 5: Retirement Planning

Retirement planning is essential to ensure financial security in your later years. It involves setting goals, understanding different retirement accounts, calculating how much you need to save, and creating a plan to achieve those savings.

Aging Clients: When planning for the financial future within elderly customers, it is necessary to use a holistic strategy that takes into consideration numerous elements of their lives, including their medical condition, the nature of their families, and their personal objectives. As financial advisers work with customers who are getting older, the following have been some important things to keep in mind. Assisting clients in determining the possibility that they may require long-term care and developing a strategy for paying for the costs of such care, whether using insurance coverage, savings, or other means, is the first step in the long-term care planning process.

Estate arranging: Assist clients in drafting or revising their powers of attorney, trusts, and other estate planning instruments to guarantee that their assets are dispersed in accordance with their preferences and to minimize the impact of any potential tax implications.

Financial planning: Review the clients' retirement savings and investment plans to ensure that they have sufficient income to maintain their lifestyle throughout retirement. This includes taking into consideration the possibility of rising healthcare costs and inflation.

Costs for healthcare: Discuss the potential impact that clients' healthcare expenses may have on their financial situation, including Medicare coverage, additional insurance alternatives, including long-term care insurance.

Social Security and pension optimization: Assist clients in maximizing their Social Security benefits and in making well-informed judgments regarding the timing of their benefits claims depending on their specific circumstances. Help clients understand their pension options and how they fit into their total retirement income plan. In a similar vein, aid clients in understanding their pension possibilities.

Asset protection: Put in place procedures to preserve the assets of your customers against potential dangers, such as the costs of long-term care, lawsuits, and creditors.

Work with clients to reduce their tax responsibilities during retirement by utilizing tax-efficient investment strategies and retirement account disbursements. This is part of the tax planning process.

Aiding customers who may be responsible for the financial well-being of elderly parents or other family members by assisting them in navigating difficult legal and financial issues is the eighth step in providing financial caregiving.

Planning for end-of-life care involves assisting clients in making significant choices on end-of-life care, such as advance directives, powers of attorney, and funeral arrangements.

Regular reviews and adjustments: It is important to examine and amend the financial plans of your clients on a regular basis to consider any changes that may occur in their health, family status, market conditions, or tax legislation.

It is crucial for financial advisers to approach these talks with empathy, sensitivity, and respect for their clients' autonomy and individual choices. This is in addition to the fact that they are responsible for delivering financial guidance. Developing a sense of trust and connection with elderly customers is essential to assist them in feeling at ease while expressing their worries regarding their finances and making significant choices regarding their future.

Retirement goals: Money saved to retire, retirement accounts, 401(k)s, IRAs, Defined Pension Plan, and Defined Contribution Plan.

Strategies for Retirement Planning: Determine when to start: The earlier a person starts planning, the more time this person's money must grow.

Estimate how much money you will need: This step involves calculating how much money you will need to maintain your current lifestyle in retirement. You can talk with a financial advisor, or you can use online retirement calculators to help you estimate the amount you will need.

Set priorities: This step involves deciding what is most important to you in retirement. For example, you may want to travel or spend more time with your family. By working with a financial advisor and knowing your priorities can help you make professional decisions about your retirement plan.

Choose accounts: There are many types of retirement accounts available, such as 401(k)s, IRAs, and Roth IRAs. Each has its own advantages and disadvantages, so it is important to choose the right one(s) for your needs.

Choose investments: once you have chosen your retirement accounts, you will need to decide how to invest your money. Generally, financial advisors will do a risk analysis of an individual to see what their risk tolerance is, such as whether they are risk takers, risk advisors, risk advisors, risk averters, risk indifferent.

We may seek the advice of a financial counselor to maximize our pension contribution, which is a method that is typically implemented by employers. Utilizing the pension benefits that are available to the individual, as well as their spouse or beneficiaries, in the most effective manner possible is the objective of the pension maximizing strategy. As a rule, it operates as follows:

Alternatives for retirement: Once people reach retirement age, they frequently find themselves in the position of having to select from among several kinds of pension options that are provided by their company. An annuity for a single life, an annuity for a joint and survivor, or a lump sum payment are all possible choices among these alternatives.

Assessment of choices: When individuals maximize their pensions, they analyze the various options that are accessible to them and take into consideration a variety of criteria, including their own individual life expectancy, the average lifespan of the spouse's spouse, and the monetary needs of the people they leave behind.

Choosing the option that offers the greatest payments: As opposed to automatically selecting the jointly owned and survivor of the annuity, which usually gives a lower monthly payment but continues payments to a surviving spouse after the retiree's death, the individual may choose the single life annuity, which offers a greater amount every month but stops when the retiree dies. This selection allows the person to choose the option that provides the greatest return on their investment.

Buying life insurance: A person then obtains a policy of life insurance with the additional income they receive from picking the single life annuity option to safeguard their spouse or beneficiaries if they pass away first. With the joint and survivor annuity, the death benefit of the policy would take the place of the pension payments that would have been continued to the beneficiaries after the death of the policyholder.

The price of the life insurance coverage is compared to the additional income that is received from selecting the single life annuity option. This option is done to calculate the cost-effectiveness of the financial decision. The objective is to have the increased income be more than the cost of the life insurance premiums, which will result in a surplus that can be distributed to the individual or to their beneficiaries.

Modifications over time: As people's situations change, such as their health, financial demands, or life expectancy, they may need to reevaluate their plan for maximizing their pension and adjust in accordance with the new circumstances.

The maximum of one's retirement can be a difficult strategy that calls for careful consideration of a variety of criteria, such as one's life expectancy, financial requirements, amount of risk tolerance, and the cost of insurance. In many cases, it is suggested that you obtain counsel from financial experts or retirement planners to ascertain whether the practice of pension maximization is suitable for your circumstances.

Remember, retirement planning is a process, not a one -time event. It is important to review your plan regularly and adjust as needed, however, if you are not sure where to start, consider hiring a financial

advisor.

Chapter 6: Tax Planning:

Tax planning is a crucial part of financial management, and understanding the many parts of taxes, tax-efficient investing, and tax-advantaged accounts can help people optimize their economic strategies. Here is an overview:

Understanding Taxes:

Income tax: This is the tax on the money you earn, which can be from various sources such as salary, business income, or investment gains.

Capital Gains Tax: This is levied on the profits from the sale of investments such as stocks, bonds, or real estate.

Dividends Tax: Tax on earnings received from investments over what is paid and decided by the company board of directors.

Efficient Tax Investing:

Asset Location: Placing investments strategically across taxable and tax-advantaged accounts can lessen tax liabilities.

Tax-Advantaged Accounts:

Individual Retirement Accounts (IRAs): Traditional and Roth IRAs provide tax advantages for retirement savings.

401(k) and other Employer-Sponsored Plans allow for tax-deferred contributions and matching in some incidences.

Health Saving Accounts (HSAs): Contributions are tax-deferred, contributions are tax-deductible and can be withdrawn for tax-free qualified medical expenses.

Tax Planning Strategies:

Maximizing Deductions: Utilizing deductions like mortgage interest, charitable contributions, and educational expenses.

Timing of Income and Expenses: Adjusting the timing of income and expenses to tax advantage your tax bracket.

Two distinct types of retirement savings vehicles are available in the United States: qualified retirement plans and nonqualified retirement plans. Each of these plans has its own set of regulations and advantages. To better understand the fundamental distinctions between them, below is a breakdown: First, the tax treatment:

Qualified Plans include 401(k)s, 403(b)s, and individual retirement accounts (IRAs), which are examples of eligible plans that allow for contributions to the plan to be deducted from your tax returns. A reduction in your current tax due is the result of contributions deducted from your taxable income in the same year they were made. To add insult to injury, the gains on investments made within the plan are tax-deferred, meaning you only must pay taxes once you remove the money.

Non-qualified Plans mean that you have already paid taxes on the money you contribute to the plan. On the other hand, the appreciation of the investments held within these plans is tax-deferred until they are withdrawn.

Limits on Contributions:

Qualified Plans have specified contribution limits the Internal Revenue Service establishes with each passing year. The annual contribution limit for 401 (k) was $20,500 for individuals under 50 in 2023, while it was $27,000 for those fifty or older.

Non-qualified Plans do not have the same upper limits on contributions as qualified plans. It is possible, however, that the corporation will impose certain limitations or restrictions.

Top Hat Plan is especially proper regarding CEO salary and corporate governance.

Plan of the Top Hat:

A Top Hat Plan called a "Top-Hat" plan, is a deferred compensation plan that does not require employees to meet specific qualifications. As supplemental retirement savings, these plans are often made available by businesses to high-paid employees or essential leaders from the company.

A few high-ranking personnel, typically CEOs deemed "at the top" of the organization's structure, are the target audience for these strategies, where the moniker "Top Hat" originates.

In contrast to qualified retirement plans (like 401(k) plans), Top Hat plans do not provide the same type of tax benefits to either the business or the employee. The Employee Retirement Income Security Act (ERISA), which is the law that controls most retirement plans, does not apply to them. Thus, they are free from many rules and restrictions.

Providing additional retirement benefits in addition to those available through regular employee retirement plans are one of the most common ways organizations use Top Hat Plans to recruit and keep top talent.

Handcuff plans are figurative terms, "handcuff" is used in finance and corporate governance to refer to contractual or legal restrictions that constrain the actions or behaviors of an individual.

As a means of ensuring that executives continue to be dedicated to the firm and aligned with shareholder interests, handcuffs are frequently utilized in the context of executive compensation and employment agreements.

Eld of executive compensation and A non-compete clause, which prevents executives from working for competitors for a certain period after leaving the company, or a vesting schedule for stock options or other forms of equity compensation, which require executives to remain with the company for a certain period before they can fully exercise their rights to the equity, are two examples of the various forms that these handcuffs can take.

In addition to providing stability and continuity in leadership, handcuffs aim to incentivize executives to act in a manner that benefits the firm and its shareholders.

For attracting and retaining essential personnel, as well as aligning the interests of executives with those of the firm and its shareholders, Top Hat Plans and handcuffs are both methods utilized in corporate governance.

Rules Regarding Withdrawals:

The withdrawal of funds from qualifying plans is subject to several rules and limits specific to the plan. Before reaching fifty-nine and a half, withdrawing funds from these plans is generally only possible without a 10% early withdrawal penalty. However, there are several exceptions to this rule. After 59 and a half years, withdrawals are subject to taxation as regular income.

Participation of Your Employer:

Qualified Plans: Employers frequently provide and sponsor qualified plans and may match employee contributions to a preset amount. Qualified plans are a type of retirement plan.

Non-qualified Plans are primarily reserved for high-earning employees or executives and are not typically made available to the low-wage employees' population. Non-qualified plans are plans that are not qualified. These plans are frequently tailored to the individual's needs and may or may not include payments from the employer.

Qualified Plans: Qualified plans are subject to the laws included in the Employee Retirement Income Security Act (ERISA). These regulations require plan sponsors to comply with fiduciary standards and reporting obligations to ensure the safety of plan participants.

Plans that are not qualified are exempt from the rules imposed by the Employee Retirement Income Security Act (ERISA), which allows for greater flexibility in terms of plan design and administration. Both qualified and nonqualified retirement plans offer tax advantages for retirement savings; however, qualified plans have a more favorable tax treatment upfront, stricter contribution limits and withdrawal limitations, and are subject to ERISA regulations. In conclusion, qualified plans offer more advantageous tax treatment than non-qualified plans. However, non-qualified plans may provide a different amount of tax benefits or employer engagement than qualified plans, but they allow more flexibility in contributions and withdrawals.

Required Minimum Distributions:

According to the Secure Act, the Required Minimum Distributions (RMDs) are the minimum sums that retirement plan account holders must withdraw from their accounts each year, starting at a specific age. The IRS mandates these distributions and governs all tax-deferred retirement accounts, including Traditional Individual Retirement Accounts (IRAs), SEP Individual Retirement Accounts (IRAs), SIMPLE Individual Retirement Accounts (IRAs), 401(k) Plans, 403(b) Plans, and similar accounts.

If the retirement account owner is still employed, that fact is one of the variables considered when deciding the age at which RMDs must commence. The account owner must initiate the required minimum distributions (RMDs) by April 1 of the calendar year, succeeding the year in which the account owner reaches the age of seventy-two. Retirement accounts that fall under this category include 401(k)s and individual retirement accounts. Suppose the account holder is employed and does not own a five percent share in the company that sponsors the retirement plan. In that case, they can delay the required minimum distributions (RMDs) until they achieve retirement age.

The Required Minimum Distribution is calculated by adding the life expectancy factor, which the Internal Revenue Service provides, and then subtracting the account balance from the previous year from the current year. This process provides the required minimum distribution. Every year, individuals who have retirement accounts are required to take out a specific amount of money and pay the taxes that are associated with it. This is accomplished by implementing the required minimum distributions, also known as RMDs. The account will be penalized if the required minimum distribution (RMD) is met. You may be exposed to significant fines if you do not accept your required minimum distributions (RMDs) monthly. If the required minimum distribution (RMD) was not accepted, the penalty was fifty percent of the amount that should have been withdrawn but was not. When an RMD is not taken, the consequence follows. Additionally, this penalty is levied on top of the regular income tax that would otherwise be due on the payout. In other words, the distribution is subject to both taxes. People with retirement funds should know how much money they need to withdraw from their accounts each year and save it to comply with the Internal Revenue Service's requirements and avoid penalties. The acronym for this is "required minimum distribution," or RMD for short. These actions will ensure that they are adhering to the guidelines and will assist them in avoiding any fines that may be imposed. Many financial companies handle retirement accounts that can help calculate and arrange required minimum distributions, also known as RMDs.

Gift and Estate Tax Planning is a way to minimize taxes on wealth transfer, such as transferring money out of the estate.

Hiring a Tax Professional:

Getting advice from tax professionals can provide ways for individuals to handle their financial situation.

It is important to remember that tax laws change, and you must review your situation regularly with your tax professional or financial advisor.

Kind of Mortgages:

Given the growing number of individuals who are graduating with degrees in business, finance planning, and designations, these two authors think that individuals will be able to maintain their financial stability and amass wealth if they know the many forms of mortgages. The various kinds of mortgages are adjustable, fixed, and reverse. A summary of the three most prevalent kinds is as follows: A loan with an adjustable rate, often called an ARM, is a type of mortgage in which the interest rate is subject to periodic changes based on a particular monetary list, like the prime rate or the Treasury bill rate. In most cases, these modifications occur annually following the conclusion of an introductory fixed-rate period that can range from one to fifteen years. One of the many advantages of ARMs is that their starting interest rates are typically lower than those of fixed-rate mortgages. This makes them appeal to borrowers who intend to relocate or renegotiate their mortgage within a few years. However, once the first-time fixed interest rates have passed, the interest rate may increase, which may result in increased monthly payments. A Fixed Rate: a mortgage with a fixed rate; the interest rate does not change during the overall loan term, which is often 15, 20, or 30 years. Because of this, your monthly payments for both interest and principal will remain the same throughout the loan, providing you with predictability and security. Homeowners have a widespread preference for fixed-rate mortgages because they assure them that their monthly payments will remain the same during their mortgage, regardless of fluctuations in the economy or interest rates. There is no requirement for a credit check or verification of how a homeowner paid to qualify for a reverse mortgage. This sort of mortgage is reserved for homeowners who are sixty-two years old or older.

On the other hand, if the homeowner were to reside in the house while also providing hazard insurance for the house's value, the verification procedure would be significantly simplified. If the homeowner passed away, there would be no necessity for the homeowner to make monthly mortgage payments; instead, the lender would take possession of the house. On the other hand, the homeowner's heirs could pay off the mortgage and be beneficiaries of the residence.

Chapter 7: Types of Financial Planning

Insurance and Risk Management

The Kinds of Life Insurance Policies:

Whole Life Insurance: the insured are covered for life, and premiums are usually paid for the life of the insured insurance policy, and the face amount plus proceeds are paid at death to the beneficiary named on the policy.

Term Insurance: a term policy is a policy where the premiums are less than other life insurance policies for a specified period for which the insured is covered. This could be 10,15, 20, or even 30 years. The premium usually remains the same during the policy term. When the term expires, most policies can convert the policy to another form of insurance, such as a whole life or universal life policy.

Universal Life Insurance combines the features of a whole life and term. It can keep a person insured for their entire life and will be less expensive than a whole-life policy. The interest the policy earns is based on the United States Treasury Bill, which varies monthly or yearly. The policy can build cash value, and the cash amount can be extremely high if the insured pays more than the premium amount to keep the insurance enforced. Universal Life is an excellent vehicle if a person wants to save money and have insurance protection for the rest of their life.

Variable Life Insurance: a form of whole life insurance that protects the insured's life and pays the beneficiary the policy's proceeds when the insured dies. This type of insurance is the most expensive. It builds cash value by allowing the policy owner to allocate a portion of the premium dollar to be placed in a separate account comprising various instruments, such as investment funds and bond issues. Because of its risks, variable life insurance policies are considered securities contracts regulated under federal securities laws; therefore, they must be sold with a prospectus. However, a variable insurance policy can make a lot of money or lose a lot of money.

Endowment Insurance: collects a specific premium over some time and is a convenient and easy means of providing for old age. An endowment insurance policy pays the face amount plus proceeds when the stipulated number of years, such as 15 or 20 years, is up and the insured no longer has insurance.

Annuities are periodic payments made during a fixed period that protect against the risk of outliving one's income. They are mainly purchased by older people seeking to convert capital from gratuity funds and policy maturing benefits into income for life; these are long-term growth vehicles that offer specific advantages for retirement.

Kinds of Disability Insurance

Disability policies can be purchased in a variety of ways, each of which is intended to offer financial safeguards if an individual becomes disabled and is unable to contribute to society through employment. Examples of frequent types of disability insurance include the following:

 Short-Term Disability Insurance: A policy is a type of insurance that usually offers coverage for a limited time, typically lasting for a few weeks to several months, following an accident or sickness that renders the policyholder unable to work. A person's benefits are often calculated as a percentage of their pay.

Long-Term Disability Insurance: Once the short-term coverage has expired, the long-term disability insurance coverage will begin. However, depending on the insurance terms, it may continue to offer benefits for a more extended period, even up until retirement. Benefits are calculated as a fraction of the individual's pay; however, there may be a maximum amount.

Numerous employers include disability insurance as a component of their employee benefits package. This type of insurance is known as employer-sponsored disability insurance. These plans could be either short-term, long-term, or both, and the coverage and benefits could differ based on the employment contract.

Individual Disability Insurance: Individuals can obtain disability insurance plans from insurance companies on their own from the insurance companies. Customized coverage is provided by such policies, which can be adapted to meet the needs of a person and their current financial situation for a period, usually thirty days to two years.

Individuals with impairments who cannot work can receive payments from the Social Security Disability Insurance (SSDI) program, owned and operated by the federal government. An individual's work history and the degree of their condition are considered when determining eligibility.

Employer-Sponsored Disability Insurance:

Employee-sponsored plans are policies that employees can purchase that will pay them up to sixty percent of their salary in pre-tax funds. The benefits you receive are taxed to the employee, who is responsible for paying taxes on those benefits. An elimination period usually lasts anywhere from thirty days to two years. You will start receiving benefits from a policy at this point.

Supplemental Disability Insurance: To guarantee that they are provided with adequate security if they become disabled, some people may decide to complement the disability coverage they already have with extra insurance plans.

Since each kind of disability cover has its own set of qualifying requirements, insurance limits, waiting periods, and benefit levels, it is imperative to carefully understand the conditions of any policy before acquiring it or relying on it for coverage.

Hospitalization: In most cases, hospitalization insurance, which is often referred to as health insurance or medical insurance, is available in a variety of forms, each of which is meant to cater to a particular set of requirements and expectations. Here are some examples of common types:

One sort of health insurance is known as individual health insurance, which individuals purchase to cover the cost of medical care. Coverage and price vary greatly depending on age, health status, and the requested advantages.

Many employers or organizations offer group hospitalization insurance plans to their employees or members. This type of coverage is known as "group hospitalization insurance." Since the risk is distributed across a larger population, it typically provides more generous coverage and less expensive premiums than individual policies.

Medicare: a federal government hospitalization plan that serves those who are 65 years old, as well as specific younger individuals who are disabled and individuals who have reached the age of total disability. Part A (hospital insurance), Part B (medical insurance), Part C (Medicare Advantage), and Part D (comprehensive coverage for prescription drugs) are the several components that make up this program.

Medicaid: a collaborative effort between the federal government and the states to provide health insurance to families and individuals with low incomes. Eligibility requirements and coverage differ from state to state.

Individuals in a transition period, such as unemployment or waiting for other coverage to begin, are eligible for short-term health insurance, which offers temporary coverage for their medical needs. This type of coverage is not considered comprehensive because it often provides only a restricted range of benefits.

A catastrophic health insurance plan protects against significant medical catastrophes, such as severe illness or injury. Catastrophic health insurance policies typically have cheaper rates but high deductibles.

Compared to standard health plans, high-deductible health plans (HDHPs) typically offer cheaper premiums, but their deductibles are more significant than traditional health plans. Health Savings Accounts (HSAs), which enable individuals to save money for eligible medical expenses without being subject to taxation, are frequently seen in conjunction with these accounts.

Health insurance policies referred to as supplemental health insurance offer supplementary coverage for treatments or expenses not covered by primary health insurance. A few examples of such insurance policies are dental, vision, and critical sickness coverage.

When it comes to medical expenses that may arise while traveling or residing in a foreign country, international health insurance offers coverage. Additional travel-related benefits, such as repatriation and emergency medical evacuation, could be included with this package.

To discover the hospitalization insurance plan most suitable for your requirements and financial constraints, it is vital to thoroughly analyze and compare the terms, coverage, and exclusions of the various options available to you.

Property and Casualty Insurance plays a crucial role in financial planning by protecting against various risks. Here are some key types of property and casualty insurance that are essential for financial planning:

Homeowners Insurance: covers damage to the insured's home and personal property and provides liability protection in case someone is injured on the property.

Auto Insurance: covers damage to the insured vehicle and liability for bodily injury or property damage caused by the insured while driving.

Renters Insurance: protects the personal property of renters and provides liability coverage.

Identity Theft Insurance: a form of protection that safeguards individuals from fraudulent activity on their bank accounts, credit cards, and identification documents; this protection is beneficial for preserving your credit score.

Umbrella Insurance offers additional liability coverage beyond the limits of their insurance policies and provides broader protection in case of major claims or lawsuits.

Flood Insurance covers damage to property caused by floods, typically not covered under standard homeowners or renters' insurance.

Earthquake Insurance: protects against damage to property caused by earthquakes, as standard policies usually exclude this coverage.

Business Insurance: includes various policies such as property insurance, liability insurance, and business interruption insurance to protect businesses from financial losses.

Liability Insurance: offers protection against claims of injury or damage to third parties for which the insured is responsible.

Professional Liability Insurance, also known as errors and omissions insurance, protects professionals against negligence or inadequate work claims.

Workers' Compensation Insurance: covers medical expenses and lost wages for employees injured or ill while on the job.

Cyber Insurance: protects against losses related to cyberattack data breaches and other cyber threats.

Boat and Yacht Insurance: covers damage to ships or yachts and provides liability protection for accidents on the water.

Travel Insurance offers coverage for unexpected events and during travel, such as trip cancellations, medical emergencies, and lost baggage.

Including these types of property and casualty insurance in your financial plan helps mitigate the economic impact of unforeseen events, protecting both your assets and your liability exposure. It is important to assess individual needs and risks when planning insurance coverage.

Assessing and Managing Risk

Assessing and managing risk is crucial to decision-making and planning in various domains, including business, finance, project management, and more. Here are some general principles and steps involved in the process:

Risk Identification:

Identify potential risks that could affect your objectives.

Categorize risks into different types, such as strategic, operational, financial, and compliance risks.

Risk Management involves various strategies to handle potential risks systematically. The four common risk management strategies are:

Avoidance: This strategy aims to eliminate the risk or withdraw from activities that pose a potential danger. It involves not engaging in certain activities or practices that could lead to negative consequences.

Transfer: Risk transfer involves shifting the impact of a risk to another party. This can be done through contracts, insurance, or other financial arrangements. By transferring the risk, an organization can share the burden with another entity.

Retention: Retaining risk means accepting and dealing with potential consequences internally. This strategy is chosen when the cost of transferring or avoiding the risk is higher than managing it within the organization's capacity.

Reduction: Risk reduction involves taking actions to decrease the likelihood or impact of a risk. This can be achieved through implementing safety measures, improving processes, or investing in technologies that mitigate the potential adverse outcomes.

In practice, organizations often use a combination of these strategies to effectively manage risks based on their nature, impact, and feasibility of implementation. Each strategy has advantages and limitations, and the choice depends on the organization's specific circumstances and risk appetite.

Risk Evaluation:

Determine whether the level of risk is acceptable or if further action is needed.

Consider the organization's risk appetite and tolerance.

Contingency Planning:

Develop contingency plans for high-priority risks.

Prepare responses to potential scenarios to minimize the impact.

Communication and Reporting:

Communicate risk information to relevant stakeholders.

Provide regular reports on the status of risk management efforts.

Adaptability:

Be flexible and adapt risk management strategies as the business environment evolves.

Continuously reassess and update risk management processes.

Training and Awareness:

Employers must be aware of accidents and disabilities of their employees by providing workers compensation insurance for employees, also they must provide coverage for stakeholders in case they get injured on the premises.

Foster a risk-aware culture within the organization.

Remember that the specific approach to risk management may vary based on the industry, organization size, and the nature of the activities involved. Regularly reviewing and updating risk management practices is essential to staying resilient in the face of uncertainties. Other kinds of insurance are crucial for protecting and sustaining a business are keyman insurance for life and disability in the event of death or disability.

Chapter 8: Estate Planning

Estate Planning Basics

Estate planning, wills, trusts, and inheritance and legacy planning are interconnected aspects of managing assets and ensuring a smooth transfer of wealth to future generations. Let us integrate the basics of these concepts:

Assessments:

Evaluate your assets, including properties, investments, and personal belongings.

Consider your financial goals, family situation, and healthcare preferences.

Legal Documents:

Create essential legal documents, including a will, power of attorney, and healthcare directives.

Reverse Mortgage: a popular loan that individuals can get from their home's equity up to a percentage of their financial needs. With a few requirements, they must carry fire insurance to protect the lender's interest at the homeowner's death. The home goes to the lender unless a family decides to pay the loan balance. Two advantages are that the homeowner does not need to do a credit check or pay off the loan.

Beneficiary Designation:

Review and update beneficiary designations on life insurance, retirement accounts, and other assets.

Guardianship:

Designate guardians for minor children in case both parents pass away.

Debt and Tax Considerations:

Address how debts and taxes will be handled in your estate plan.

Explore strategies to minimize estate taxes.

Regular review and updates:

Review and adjust legacy plans periodically based on changing family dynamics, laws, and financial situations.

Look Back Period:

In the environment of nursing homes, the term "look back period" frequently pertains to the period during which a person's financial transactions and assets are examined to determine whether they are eligible for Medicaid assistance for long-term healthcare, which includes nursing home care.

It is a healthcare program owned and operated jointly by the federal government and the states in the United States. Its purpose is to provide low-income people with health coverage, which includes coverage for long-term care services such as nursing home care. The Medicaid program, on the other hand, has stringent qualifications, notably in terms of income and assets.

When applying for Medicaid, when an individual has engaged in specific financial activities, such as transferring property to relatives or establishing trusts, Medicaid can impose a penalty period during which the applicant is ineligible for benefits. This punishment may last for a period. The duration of this penalty period is established by considering the worth of the property that was transferred and the cost of nursing home care in the individual's locality.

The "look back period" refers to the period before the Medicaid application and is used to examine the financial activities. On average, the look-back period in the United States is sixty months; however, this might vary from state to state. This indicates that Medicaid will investigate any financial dealings that the individual or their spouse engaged in during the five years immediately before the application for Medicaid.

Before considering Medicaid eligibility for nursing home care, it is crucial for families and individuals to have a thorough understanding of the look-back period and to plan for it properly. This is because specific financial activities performed throughout this period can directly affect eligibility and result in punishment periods. When navigating the complexity of Medicaid eligibility and the look-back period, it can be helpful to seek the advice of a knowledgeable law attorney or a financial adviser specializing in healthcare preparation.

Wills:

Draft a will to specify how your assets should be distributed after death.

Appoint an executor and address guardianship for minor children.

Trusts:

Consider creating trusts for specific purposes, such as avoiding probate, minimizing taxes, and managing assets for beneficiaries.

Choose between revocable and irrevocable trusts based on your goals.

Probate Avoidance:

Understand that assets held in trusts may avoid probate, providing a more efficient and private transfer of assets.

Flexibility:

Recognize that trusts offer more flexibility in addressing complex family situations and long-term asset management.

Privacy:

Trusts generally offer more privacy as they are not part of the public probate process.

Comprehensive Planning:

Using both wills and trusts in a comprehensive estate plan is expected, each serving specific purposes.

Inheritance and Legacy Planning:

Family Communication:

Facilitate open communication with family members about financial matters, values, and expectations.

Values and Visions:

Clearly articulate personal values and establish a vision for the family's legacy.

Consider creating a family mission statement reflecting shared values.

Charitable Givings:

Include charitable giving as part of the legacy plan.

Establish foundations or trusts for ongoing charitable contributions.

Education and Guidance:

Provide education on managing wealth for future generations.

117

Seek professional advice from financial planners, estate planning attorneys, and tax professionals.

Documenting Personal History:

Write legacy letters or create documents sharing personal experiences, values, and life lessons.

Preserve family history through various means.

Memorialization:

Leave specific gifts or instructions for memorializing individuals or the family.

Professional Guidance:

Consult with an estate planning attorney and financial advisors to ensure legal and financial compliance.

Consider engaging in collaborative philanthropic projects as a family.

In summary, integrating estate planning basics, wills, trusts, and inheritance and legacy planning involves a comprehensive approach considering financial and non-financial aspects. Professional guidance and open communication with family members are crucial in creating a plan that aligns with your values and goals. Regular reviews ensure that the plan remains relevant as circuit

Chapter 9: Financial Planning for Special Situations

Financial planning for special situations requires careful consideration of unique circumstances that may impact an individual's or a family's financial well-being. Here are some key aspects to address in special situations:

Divorce:

Asset Division: Understand the financial implications of dividing assets and liabilities.

Alimony and Child Support: Plan for potential obligations or entitlements.

Update Legal Documents: Revise wills, trusts, and beneficiary designations.

Marriage:

Joint Financial Goals: Establish shared financial goals and strategies.

Prenuptial Agreement: Consider a prenup for asset protection and clarity on financial matters.

Birth or Adoption:

Budget Adjustment: Update the budget to account for new expenses related to raising a child.

Insurance Review: Consider life insurance and update beneficiaries.

Loss of a Loved One:

Estate Settlement: Understand the process of settling the deceased's estate.

Life Insurance Claims: Initiate claims and review beneficiaries.

Financial Assistance Programs: Explore potential financial assistance programs.

Disability:

Insurance Coverage: Ensure adequate disability insurance coverage.

Emergency Funds: Establish or review an emergency fund to cover unexpected expenses.

Legal Documents: Update legal documents to include disability provisions.

Career Change or Job Loss:

Budget Adjustment: Adjust the budget based on changes in income.

Emergency Fund: Rely on an emergency fund during the transition.

Retirement Accounts: Consider rolling over retirement accounts from previous employers.

Windfall (Inheritance, Lottery, etc.):

Financial Planning: Develop a comprehensive plan considering taxes, investments, and long-term goals.

Professional Advice: Consult financial advisors to make informed decisions.

Health Crisis:

Health Insurance: Ensure adequate health insurance coverage.

Medical Expenses: Plan for potential medical expenses and consider health savings accounts (HSAs).

Legal Documents: Review and update legal documents to address health-related decisions.

Starting a Business:

Business Plan: Develop a detailed business plan, including financial projections.

Emergency Fund: Maintain a personal emergency fund while starting the business.

Insurance Needs: Consider business insurance and protect personal assets.

Educational Expenses:

529 Plans: Explore tax-advantaged 529 plans for education savings.

Scholarships and Grants: Research and apply for available scholarships and grants.

Student Loans: Plan for student loan repayment and explore repayment options.

Tax Changes:

Tax Planning: Adjust financial plans in response to changes in tax laws.

Professional Assistance: Consult with tax professionals for personalized advice.

Global Events (Pandemics, Economic Crises):

Emergency Fund: Strengthen emergency funds to navigate uncertain times.

Investment Strategy: Review and adjust investment portfolios based on changing economic conditions.

Government Assistance Programs: Explore available government assistance programs.

In special situations, seeking professional advice from financial planners, lawyers, or tax professionals becomes crucial. Adapting financial plans and making informed decisions is essential to navigating the complexities of unique life circumstances. Regular reviews and updates to financial plans ensure they remain aligned with changing needs and goals.

The form of a corporation that, for federal taxation purposes, decides to pass through to its owners the income, losses, deductions, and credits that are incurred by the corporation when it is subject to taxes. Any corporate entity is broken down into the following categories, with thorough explanations:

The individual or individuals must decide what form of business would work best, such as the ones listed below:

In business entities, the sole proprietorship is the most basic format. A sole proprietorship is the simplest and most fundamental kind of enterprise, as it is owned and operated by a single individual for the duration of its existence.

The owner continues to exercise complete authority over the business and has a right to get all the profits.

The legal owner of the firm is personally accountable for all the company's obligations and debts, as they are all the owner's responsibility.

Primarily, the owner's responsibility is to file their taxes on their tax return (for information regarding taxes in the United States, please refer to the Schedules.

One sort of partner is known as a general partnership, and it can be described by the fact that two or more individuals jointly own shares of the company and manage the business.

It is the partners' responsibility to divide the earnings, damages, and responsibilities between themselves by the laws of your case. Shareholders can take on a particular level of responsibility for the company's debts and liabilities; nevertheless, this duty is not unlimited.

According to the Internal Revenue Service (IRS), it is necessary to comply with a few limits and requirements.

The company, a separate legal body that the owners own, is called a C corporation. Only a restricted amount of responsibility for the debts and obligations of the company is allocated to the shareholders. A C corporate income tax applies to C corporations at both the federal and state levels when they are taxed. To the extent the corporation desires, the number of stockholders can be as great as ever.

Their organizational structure is more intricate than that of other business entities, and they are subject to more regulatory duties than other business entities.

When it comes to business entities, virtually every kind of company has its own set of advantages and disadvantages, and the decision between them is based on a few factors, such as protection from responsibility, the repercussions of taxes, the hierarchy of management, and the profit objectives that are being pursued. When selecting which type of company entity is most appropriate for a joint venture agreement, seeking help from an attorney or a financial advisor specializing in the legal and economic fields is vital.

If the partnership incurs obligations or liabilities, it is the responsibility of each partner to pay off those debts and liabilities personally. Payments are typically required to be filed on the partners' personal tax returns, while the partnership itself is required to file an informational return that includes tax information.

The following are examples of limited liability companies (LLCs):

An organizational structure that combines features of a corporation with those of a partnership or sole proprietorship to establish a combination business structure.

Owners are referred to as "members" and have limited accountability for the assets and liabilities of the limited liability company (LLC).

The power to choose whether to be taxed as a sole proprietorship, partnership (pass-through taxes), or corporation.

A management structure that is more flexible and has fewer complexities than corporations' management structures.

An S-Corp can have no more than 100 shareholders. However, there are some exceptions and additional rules that apply to certain types of shareholders, such as family members and Employee Stock Ownership Plans (ESOPs).

Financial Planning for Marriage: Before getting into a marriage, take some time to define short-term and long-term goals for yourself as a couple. This may include savings, home ownership, and emergency savings, and should be 3 to 6 months of rent or mortgage payments.

Financial Planning for Children's Education: Prepare yourself for the cost of education, which includes books, living expenses, and tuition. It is also essential for children to excel academically to increase their chances of receiving scholarships and grants.

Financial Planning for Divorce: You must have a clear understanding of your financial situation, including assets, debts, and expenses. This will be crucial during your proceedings.

Chapter 10: Monitoring and Adjusting Your Plan

Monitoring and adjusting your financial plan are critical to ensuring its effectiveness and relevance over time. Financial situations, goals, and external factors can change, requiring regular reviews and adjustments. Here is a guide on how to monitor and adapt your financial plan:

Regular Reviews:

Frequency: Notes should be made on the calendar semi-annually or annually. Most of the time, frequent reviews may be necessary in case of significant changes in life, and financial planning tools are needed to prompt reviews.

Life Changes:

Some events will impose specific financial planning changes, such as marriage, divorce, birth, death, career, or relocation.

Financial Goals: Review and adjust financial goals based on changing circumstances.

Income and Expenses:

Income Changes: Update your plan to reflect changes in income, including salary increases, bonuses, or decreases.

Expense Tracking: Regularly track expenses to identify any deviations from the budget and adjust accordingly.

Investment Portfolios:

Market Conditions: Monitor market conditions and assess the performance of your investment portfolio.

Risk Tolerance: Reevaluate your risk tolerance and adjust investments accordingly.

Diversification: Ensure your investment portfolio remains diversified to manage risk.

Emergency Funds:

Assessment: Regularly assess the adequacy of your emergency fund, especially during economic uncertainties.

Adjust Contributions: Consider adjusting contributions to the emergency fund based on changing circumstances.

Debt Management:

The process of planning and controlling your debt, as well as being able to make payments when due, is referred to as debt management services.

Interest Rates: Monitor changes in interest rates and assess the impact on your debt.

Repayment Strategies: Adjust debt repayment strategies based on financial goals and changes in income.

Insurance Coverage:

Life Changes: Update insurance coverage to align with family size, income, or assets changes.

Comparison Shopping: Periodically review insurance policies and explore opportunities for cost savings.

Retirement Planning:

Retirement Age: Reassess your retirement age and adjust contributions to retirement accounts accordingly.

Market Conditions: Consider the impact of market conditions on retirement savings and adjust as needed.

Tax Planning:

Changes in Tax Laws: Stay informed about tax laws and adjust your tax planning strategies accordingly.

Maximize Tax Benefits: Explore opportunities to maximize tax benefits, such as contributing to tax-advantaged accounts.

Estate Planning:

Legal Documents: Regularly review and update wills, trusts, and other documents to reflect current intentions.

Beneficiary Designations: Confirm that beneficiary designations are up to date.

Professional Guidance:

Financial Advisor Consultation: Schedule regular meetings with a financial advisor for professional guidance.

Legal and Tax Advice: Seek legal and tax advice, when necessary, especially during significant life changes.

Adaptability: Keeping informed about market trends, economic conditions, and industry changes is critical to review your budget regularly, prioritizing your needs, adjusting your income and expenses, setting realistic goals, track and evaluate your progress.

Flexibility: Embrace flexibility in your financial plan to accommodate unexpected changes.

Learn and Adjust: Continuously educate yourself about personal finance and adapt your plan based on new knowledge.

Record Keeping:

Organize Documents: Maintain organized records of financial documents and account statements.

Secure Storage: Store important documents securely and consider digital backups.

Emergency Adjustments:

Immediate Changes: Be prepared to make immediate adjustments in response to sudden financial challenges or opportunities.

Regular monitoring and adjustments are crucial to keeping your financial plan aligned with your goals and adapting to changing circumstances. Being proactive and staying informed contributes to the long-term success of your economic strategy.

Regularly Reviewing Your Financial Plan

Making an Adjustment as needed

Staying on Track to Achieve Your Goals

Financial planning is crucial to managing one's money and ensuring a secure financial future. The essentials of financial planning encompass various vital elements that individuals should consider when achieving their financial goals. Here is a summary of the core aspects of financial planning:

Budgeting:

Creating a budget is fundamental to financial planning. It involves tracking income, expenses, and saving for future goals.

Budgeting helps individuals understand where their money is going and enables them to make informed financial decisions.

Emergency Fund:

An emergency fund is essential for unforeseen medical emergencies or job loss.

Financial advisors usually recommend three to six months of savings in your account.

Debt Management:

Managing and reducing debt is crucial for long-term financial health treatments.

We plan to repay high-interest loans to free up resources for other financial goals.

Insurance:

Having adequate insurance coverage is a crucial element of financial planning.

This includes health, life, property and casualty insurance, and other coverages to protect against unforeseen events.

Investing:

Investing is a way to grow wealth over time. It involves putting money into multiple essential investments to spread risk and maximize returns.

Retirement Planning:

Planning for retirement involves setting aside funds to support oneself during retirement years. Contributing to retirement accounts such as 401(k)s, IRAs, and ROTH IRAs are standard vehicles used to increase your retirement for the future.

Estate Planning:

Estate planning involves preparing for the distribution of assets after death.

It includes creating a will, establishing trusts, and making decisions about inheritance and beneficiaries,

Financial Education:

Contributions to educational and financial plans are essential for saving money for your child's education and staying aligned with the rising cost of college.

In conclusion, the essentials of financial planning encompass budgeting, emergency funds, debt management, insurance, investing, retirement planning, estate planning, and ongoing financial education. By addressing these key areas, individuals can work to achieve their financial goals and build a secure financial future.

Key Takeaways:

The Essentials of Financial Planning" covers various topics crucial for effective financial planning. Here are key takeaways from the content:

Goals Setting: Clearly define short-term and long-term financial goals to guide your planning process.

Budgeting: Create a realistic budget to manage income and expenses, ensuring a balanced financial retirement for life.

Emergency Fund: Build and maintain an emergency fund to cover unexpected expenses such as medical, car, and house repairs.

Debt management: Strategically handle and reduce debt to avoid unnecessary financial burdens.

Investment Planning: Understand different investment options, risk tolerance, and diversification for optimal portfolio growth.

Retirement Planning: Plan retirement by estimating future expenses, understanding retirement accounts, and optimizing savings for a rainy day.

Insurance Coverage: Evaluate and purchase the insurance needed to protect your health, life, property, and other relevant areas.

Tax Planning: Be aware of tax implications and plan accordingly to minimize tax liabilities.

Estate Planning: Develop a comprehensive estate plan, including wills, trusts, and other relevant documents to ensure a smooth transfer of assets.

Continuous Review: At least once a year unless you have some change in your lifestyle or changes in the market.

Remember, the specifics of financial planning can vary based on individual circumstances, and it is advisable to consult with a financial advisor for professional services.

Encourage Ongoing Financial

Education: Promoting ongoing financial education is crucial for individuals to make informed financial decisions. The essentials of financial planning include budgeting, saving, investing, managing debt, and planning. You can build a strong foundation for financial success by continuously educating yourself about these topics. Consider exploring resources such as books, online courses, workshops, and credible websites. Also, you can hire a financial advisor such as a Certified Financial Planner, Chartered Financial Consultant, or Chartered Life Underwriter. They can give you good personal advice. Remember, the more knowledge you have about financial planning, the better equipped you will be to achieve your financial goals.

In sum, the importance of financial planning cannot be overemphasized because we are reminded about ENRON, which went insolvent, and the employees lost their retirement money. The two writers believe that if those employees had hired a Financial Planner to do some financial planning for them, they would have a good retirement today.

Glossary of Financial Terms

The authors have listed below words and definitions that individuals will regularly use when working on a financial plan for themselves or their businesses:

Assets: what a person has, such as a house, car, stocks, bonds, and real estate

Debt: what individuals owe, such as credit cards, cars, and house.

Loans are mortgages, and personal and credit card debt are all examples of liabilities. Liability refers to any debt or obligation that is owed by an individual or business.

Equity: ownership interest in an asset that remains after any liabilities have been subtracted. Equity is a term that refers to ownership in the form of stocks when it is used in the context of a firm.

It is common practice to indicate the cost of borrowing money as a percentage of the total amount of the loan, which is referred to as the interest rate. Investments and savings both have the potential to generate interest.

Cash or assets that are used to generate income or wealth are referred to as capital.

Stocks: are of instrument that represents ownership in a firm and is referred to as stock. Stockholders are entitled to several benefits, including voting rights at shareholder meetings and a portion of the profits made by the company.

Bonds are a type of debt investment in which an investor lends money to an entity (often something like a corporation or the government) for a predetermined amount of time at an interest rate that is either fixed or variable.

Dividends: profits from the company are the percentage of a company's profits that is distributed to its owners.

Return on investment (ROI) is the amount money that a person made on the investment. Income Statement is a type of financial statement that provides information on a company's revenues, costs, and net income during a particular time. A few of the most fundamental terminology that is utilized in the field of finance are covered in this glossary; however, there are more terms and concepts to investigate in the field of finance and investing.

The two writers have listed below words and definitions that individuals will extensively use when working on a financial plan for themselves or their businesses:

Assets: what a person has, such as a house, car, stocks, bonds, and real estate

Debt: is what individuals owe, such as a credit card, car, and a home.

146

Loans are mortgages, and personal and credit card responsibilities are all examples of liabilities. Liability refers to any debt or obligation owed by an individual or business.

Equity refers to ownership in the form of stocks when used in a firm's context.

It is a common practice to specify the cost of borrowing money as a percentage of the total amount of the loan, referred to as the interest rate. Investments and savings both have the potential to create interest.

Cash or assets used to generate income or wealth are called capital.

Stocks represent ownership in a firm and are referred to as stock.

Bonds are debt investments that lend money to an entity for a predetermined amount of time at a fixed or variable interest rate for a return.

Dividends are profits from the company's percentage of profits distributed to its owners.

Return on investment (ROI) individuals usually invest in real estate stock and bonds to receive a return on their investments.

An Income Statement provides a company with information on revenues, costs, and net income during a particular time.

A few of the most fundamental terminology utilized in the finance field are covered in this glossary; however, there are more terms and concepts to investigate in finance and investing.

Stocks represent ownership in a firm and are referred to as Stockholders. They are entitled to several benefits, including voting rights at shareholder meetings and a portion of the profits made by the company

Selected References

Altfest, L. (2004). Personal financial planning: Origins, developments, and a plan for future direction. The American Economist, 48(2), pp. 53-60.https://doi.org/10.1177/056943450404800204

Anderson, C., and Sharpe, D. L. (2008). The efficacy of life planning communication tasks in developing successful planner-client relationships, Journal of Financial Planning, 21(16), pp. 66-77.

Asebedo, S., D. (2019). Financial planning client interaction theory (FPCIT). Journal of Personal Finance, 18(1), pp. 9-23.

Asebedo, S. D., and Purdon, E. (2018). Planning for conflict in client relationships. Journal of Financial Planning, 31(10), pp. 48-56.

Christiansen, T., and DeVaney, S. A. (1998). Antecedents of trust and commitment in the financial planner-client relationship. Journal of Financial Counseling and Planning, 9(2), pp.1-10.

Dubofsky, D., and Sussman, L. (2009). The changing role of the financial planner part 1 From financial analytics to coaching and life planning. Journal of Financial Planning, 22(8),pp. 48-57.

Dubofsky, D., and Sussman, L. (2010). The bonding continuum in financial planner-client relationships. Journal of Financial Planning, 23(10), pp. 66-78.

Gennaioli, N., Shleifer, A., and Vishny, R. (2015). Money doctors. The Journal of Finance,70(1): pp. 91-114.https://doi.org/10.1111/jofi.12188

Grable, J. E., and Chatterjee, S. (2014). Reducing wealth volatility: The value of financial advice as measured by zeta. Journal of Financial Planning, 27(8), pp. 45-51.

Horwitz, E. J., and Klontz, B. (2013). Understanding and dealing with client resistance to change. Journal of Financial Planning, 26(11), pp. 27-31.

Kinniry, F. M., Jaconetti, C. M., DiJoseph, M. A., and Zilbering, Y. (2016). Putting a value on your value: quantifying Vanguard advisor's alpha. The Vanguard Group.

Kitces, M. (2016). Evaluating financial planning strategies and quantifying their economic impact. Journal of Personal Finance, 15 (2), pp. 7-28

Klontz, B., Kahler, R., and Kontz, T. (2016). Facilitating financial health: Tools for financial planners, coaches, and therapists (2nd ed.). Erlanger, KY: The National Underwriter Company Larson, R., and Edwards, B. (2014). Calculus (10th Ed.).

Boston, MA: Brooks/Cole. Lawson, D., and Klontz, B. (2017). Integrating behavioral finance, financial psychology, and financial therapy into the 6-step financial planning process, Journal of Financial Planning,30(7): pp. 48-55.

MacLeod, A. K., Coates, E., and Hetherton, J. (2008). Increasing well-being through teaching goal setting and planning skills: Results of a brief intervention. Journal of Happiness Studies, 9(2), pp. 185-196.https://doi.org/10.1007/s10902-007-9057-2

Martin, M., and Westerhof, G. J. (2003). Do you need to have them, or should you believe you have them? Resources, their appraisal, and well-being in adulthood, Journal of Adult Development, 10(2), pp. 99-112. Page 18

Prenda, K. M., and Lachman, M. E. (2001). Planning for the future: A life management strategy for increasing control and life satisfaction in adulthood. Psychology and Aging,16(2), pp. 206-216.https://doi.org/10.1037/0882-7974.16.2.206

Sussman, L., and Dubofsky, D. (2009). The changing role of the financial planner part 2: Prescriptions for coaching and life planning. Journal of Financial Planning, 22(9), pp. 50-56

www.ingramcontent.com/pod-product-compliance
Lightning Source LLC
Chambersburg PA
CBHW071856200326
41519CB00016B/4404